AI for Gig Workers, Freelancers & 1099 Income

Smart Tax Solutions for the Self-Employed

By Joe Correa

Published by Live Stronger Faster

This book is for educational and informational purposes only. The author and publisher are not engaged in rendering legal, financial, tax, or other professional advice. Readers should consult a qualified professional before making any financial decisions.

First Edition

Table of Contents

Introduction

The modern workforce has undergone one of the most radical transformations in human history, and nowhere is that more visible than in the rise of gig workers, freelancers, independent contractors, online entrepreneurs, and self-employed professionals who earn income through dozens of platforms instead of a single employer. Whether you drive for rideshare apps, sell on Amazon, create content on YouTube, freelance on Upwork, consult clients remotely, run a digital store, or earn royalties from books, music, or software, your income now flows from multiple sources, multiple countries, multiple payment processors, and multiple tax reporting systems. What once required a simple W-2 now involves 1099-NEC forms, 1099-K reports, platform statements, payment processor data, crypto transactions, expense receipts, mileage logs, and dozens of micro-transactions that together determine your true taxable income. This complexity has made self-employed taxation one of the most stressful, error-prone, and expensive financial tasks in modern life, yet it is precisely here that artificial intelligence delivers its greatest power.

For gig workers and freelancers, taxes are not just an annual filing event. They are a daily, invisible drain on cash flow, time, and mental energy. Unlike traditional employees whose taxes are automatically withheld from each paycheck, self-employed individuals must calculate, track, save, and submit their own taxes throughout the year. Every dollar you earn is technically gross income until you correctly document deductions, expenses, and business costs. Miss a deduction, misclassify an expense, forget a receipt, or underestimate your quarterly payments, and you can easily lose thousands of dollars to overpayment, penalties, or audits. This is not because the tax code is unfair, but because it was designed for businesses with accounting departments, not individuals juggling twenty platforms, five income streams, and hundreds of micro-expenses. Artificial intelligence changes this equation by turning chaos into clarity.

AI does not simply “do your taxes.” It becomes your always-on financial intelligence system that watches your money in real time, categorizes transactions automatically, flags deductible expenses, estimates quarterly tax liabilities, and even suggests strategies to legally reduce what you owe. Instead of waiting until April to discover what went wrong, AI allows freelancers and gig workers to know exactly where they stand financially at any moment. It sees patterns that humans miss, remembers rules that humans forget, and applies tax logic consistently across every dollar you earn and spend. For someone with irregular income, fluctuating expenses, and unpredictable work volume, this kind of real-time intelligence is nothing short of transformational.

One of the greatest myths about self-employment is that paying less tax requires complicated schemes or risky behavior. In reality, most freelancers overpay because they fail to claim everything they are legally entitled to. Home office deductions, internet usage, phone bills, software subscriptions, equipment depreciation, travel costs, meals, education, and even portions of rent and utilities are often deductible when properly categorized. The problem is not the lack of tax benefits; it is the lack of precision. Humans are bad at tracking thousands of small financial details across a year. AI, on the other hand, excels at exactly this task. It connects to your bank accounts, credit cards, invoicing systems, payment processors, and gig platforms, then continuously builds a complete, categorized, audit-ready financial picture that would take a human accountant hundreds of hours to assemble.

This is especially powerful in the gig economy, where income is fragmented across multiple platforms. You may earn from Uber, Airbnb, Etsy, Stripe, PayPal, Amazon, YouTube, Patreon, freelance marketplaces, and private clients all at once. Each platform reports income differently, some issue 1099s while others do not, and some provide only monthly summaries. AI systems reconcile all of this data automatically, matching deposits to sources, identifying missing income reports, and ensuring nothing is overlooked. This prevents both underreporting, which triggers audits, and overreporting, which leads to unnecessary tax payments. The result is a level of accuracy and confidence that was previously only available to large corporations.

Quarterly estimated taxes are another area where freelancers struggle. Without an employer withholding taxes automatically, self-employed individuals must guess how much to send to the IRS every three months. Guess too low and you face penalties and interest. Guess too high and you give the government an interest-free loan that drains your cash flow. AI solves this by forecasting your income, projecting your deductions, and calculating your true tax liability in real time. As your income rises or falls, your estimated payments adjust automatically. Instead of guessing, you know. Instead of hoping, you plan. This allows freelancers to keep more money working in their business instead of sitting unnecessarily with the IRS.

Beyond compliance and savings, AI also provides strategic insight that most gig workers have never had access to. It can simulate scenarios such as buying new equipment, increasing ad spending, taking on more clients, or shifting income between months, showing you how each decision affects your taxes. It can recommend whether forming an LLC or S-Corp would reduce your tax burden. It can advise on retirement contributions that lower taxable income. It can even suggest timing strategies for invoices and expenses to optimize cash flow and tax efficiency. In this way, AI becomes not just a tax tool, but a financial co-pilot guiding your entire business.

The emotional impact of this shift is just as important as the financial one. Tax anxiety is one of the biggest hidden stressors for freelancers. Not knowing how much you owe, whether you made mistakes, or whether the IRS might come knocking creates a constant background tension that affects creativity, productivity, and quality of life. AI replaces that anxiety with visibility. You can see your tax position at any time. You can prepare for obligations before they become emergencies. You can file with confidence knowing that your numbers are supported by clean, organized, verifiable data. This psychological relief alone is worth more than many of the financial savings it produces.

As you move through this book, you will see how artificial intelligence transforms every part of the freelance tax experience. You will learn how AI tracks gig income across platforms, how it identifies and maximizes deductions, how it manages quarterly payments, how it prepares audit-ready records, and how it helps you build a tax-efficient freelance business that grows without fear. Whether you earn a few thousand dollars a year on the side or operate a full-time digital enterprise, the principles in this book apply equally. AI does not care how big or small you are. It cares only about data, accuracy, and optimization.

We are entering a world where the most financially successful freelancers will not be those who work the hardest, but those who use intelligence the best. Artificial intelligence levels the playing field between solo entrepreneurs and massive corporations, giving individuals access to the same analytical power that Fortune 500 companies have used for decades. In the realm of taxes, this means fewer mistakes, lower bills, and greater control over your financial destiny. This book is your guide to that new reality. The gig economy created freedom, but AI is what will make that freedom financially sustainable, scalable, and secure.

Chapter 1

The New Economy: Why Gig Workers Need AI to Survive

The global workforce has quietly crossed a tipping point. Millions of people now earn income without employers, without offices, and without predictable paychecks. Rideshare drivers, freelance designers, YouTubers, TikTok creators, Amazon sellers, consultants, coaches, remote workers, and online entrepreneurs form a vast invisible economy that runs on apps, platforms, and digital transactions rather than time clocks and W-2s. This new economy offers unprecedented freedom, but it also comes with a hidden cost: financial complexity. Every platform pays differently, reports differently, and records income differently. Instead of one clean tax document at the end of the year, gig workers are buried under dozens of 1099 forms, payment processor statements, transaction logs, mileage records, and expense receipts that must somehow be turned into one accurate tax return. This administrative burden is now one of the biggest obstacles to financial success in the gig economy.

Traditional tax systems were never designed for this type of work. They were built for employees who receive fixed salaries and have taxes automatically withheld before money ever reaches their bank account. Freelancers and contractors, by contrast, receive every dollar first and are responsible for calculating what portion belongs to the government later. That sounds empowering, but in practice it creates risk. Without precise tracking, many gig workers either overpay because they fail to claim legitimate deductions or underpay because they miscalculate what they owe. Both scenarios are financially damaging. Overpayment quietly erodes wealth, while underpayment leads to penalties, interest, and the ever-present fear of audits. AI exists to eliminate both of these problems by providing constant financial intelligence instead of once-a-year guesswork.

The biggest tax advantage freelancers have is also their greatest weakness. Because they operate businesses, they are legally allowed to deduct a wide range of expenses that employees cannot. Internet, phone, software, computers, cameras, mileage, advertising, office space, meals, training, and even portions of housing can be deducted if they are used for business. Yet most gig workers fail to capture the full value of these deductions simply because they do not track them consistently. Receipts get lost. Transactions get mixed with personal spending. Small purchases are forgotten. AI changes this by automatically scanning every transaction and identifying which ones qualify as business expenses based on patterns, merchant types, categories, and historical behavior.

What was once invisible suddenly becomes visible, and every dollar saved compounds over time.

Another major challenge in the gig economy is income volatility. One month might bring record profits while the next feels painfully slow. This makes tax planning incredibly difficult. How much should you set aside? How much should you send to the IRS? How much can you safely spend? Without accurate forecasting, freelancers often make financial decisions based on emotion rather than data. AI replaces uncertainty with prediction. By analyzing your historical income, seasonal patterns, platform trends, and expense behavior, it can estimate future earnings and tax obligations with increasing accuracy. This allows you to budget, invest, and grow your business with confidence instead of fear.

AI also eliminates one of the most dangerous blind spots in self-employment: invisible compliance risk. Many gig workers assume that if they simply report what they see in their bank account, they are doing everything right. But tax compliance is not about what you think you earned; it is about what the IRS believes you earned based on third-party reports from platforms, payment processors, and clients. If even one of those numbers does not match your return, it raises a red flag. AI reconciles all income sources automatically, matching deposits to reported income and identifying discrepancies before they become problems. This alone can prevent audits that destroy years of financial stability.

Time is another hidden cost of freelance taxes. Manually tracking expenses, categorizing transactions, estimating quarterly payments, and preparing for filing can take dozens or even hundreds of hours per year. That is time that could be spent earning money, building a brand, or simply enjoying life. AI gives that time back. It works silently in the background, turning raw financial data into organized, compliant, and optimized tax records without constant human effort. What used to require spreadsheets and accounting software now happens automatically, accurately, and continuously.

The power of AI is not just in what it automates, but in what it reveals. Patterns emerge when thousands of transactions are analyzed together. You begin to see which clients are most profitable, which platforms generate the best returns, and which expenses are draining your income without producing value. AI allows you to treat your freelance work like a real business instead of a chaotic collection of gigs. This clarity is what separates struggling freelancers from those who build long-term wealth.

As the gig economy continues to grow, the tax system will only become more complex. Governments are increasing reporting requirements, platforms are sharing more data, and compliance standards are tightening. Those who rely on outdated manual systems will fall behind, while those who use AI will move ahead. In this new world, financial intelligence is not optional. It is the foundation of survival and success. This is why AI is no longer just a convenience for freelancers. It is their most important business tool.

"The Ledger That Never Slept"

When Maya first started freelancing as a graphic designer, she felt unstoppable. Clients from around the world paid her through PayPal, Stripe, and freelance platforms, and her bank account filled faster than it ever had when she worked a regular job. But as the months passed, the excitement slowly turned into unease. Money came in constantly, but she had no idea how much of it was really hers. Every payment felt good, yet every receipt she lost made her anxious. By the end of her first year, she faced a tax bill so large it nearly wiped out her savings, and she realized she had been flying blind.

The next year, she promised herself it would be different. She tried spreadsheets, apps, and folders of receipts, but the chaos never fully went away. One day she would forget to log a client payment. Another day she would miscategorize an expense. Small errors piled up into big mistakes. That was when she discovered an AI-powered tax system designed for freelancers.

At first it felt strange to let a machine watch her finances, but within weeks she could see everything clearly for the first time. Every dollar had a place. Every expense had a category. Nothing slipped through the cracks.

As Maya's income grew, so did the intelligence of her digital ledger. It began predicting her quarterly tax payments, showing her how much to set aside, and warning her when spending might cause a future shortfall. Instead of fearing tax season, she began preparing for it in real time. When she bought a new laptop, the AI logged it as deductible equipment. When she paid for design software, it marked it as a business expense. Even her internet bill was partially allocated to her work. What once felt overwhelming now felt effortless.

One afternoon, Maya noticed something remarkable. The AI had flagged several small expenses she had never thought about before: cloud storage, stock images, even a portion of her phone bill. Those little deductions added up to thousands of dollars by the end of the year. For the first time, she wasn't just earning more, she was keeping more. It felt like discovering money she had already worked for but never collected.

Then came the true test. One of her freelance platforms sent the IRS a report that didn't match what Maya had recorded.

Before she even noticed, the AI flagged the discrepancy and guided her through correcting it. What could have triggered an audit became a simple fix. Maya realized that her financial guardian never slept, never forgot, and never guessed. It simply knew.

By her third year, Maya no longer feared taxes. She planned around them. She invested with confidence. She even took time off knowing exactly how it would affect her income and obligations. The AI had turned her unpredictable gig work into a stable, growing business. Freedom had always brought her into freelancing, but intelligence was what finally made that freedom secure.

And in the quiet hum of algorithms and data, Maya found something she never expected in the gig economy: peace.

Chapter 2

How AI Tracks Every Dollar You Earn and Spend

In the world of gig work and self-employment, money no longer flows in simple, predictable streams. It arrives in waves, micro-payments, delayed deposits, platform balances, digital wallets, cryptocurrency transactions, and international transfers. A freelancer might receive dozens of payments in a single week, each from a different client or platform, each reported differently, and each subject to different tax rules. Traditional bookkeeping systems struggle to keep up with this complexity because they rely on human input. Artificial intelligence solves this problem by acting as a living financial map that constantly watches where money comes from, where it goes, and what it means for taxes.

AI begins its work by connecting to every place your money touches. This includes bank accounts, credit cards, invoicing systems, payment processors, gig platforms, online marketplaces, and even crypto wallets. Once connected, the system reads transaction data in real time, not just at tax season. Each deposit is analyzed to determine its source. Was it client income, a refund, a transfer, or a loan? Each expense is evaluated based on merchant type, spending history, and behavioral patterns. Was that a business meal, office supplies, software, travel, or a personal purchase? Instead of forcing you to label everything manually, the AI builds an intelligent profile of your financial behavior and applies it automatically.

What makes this possible is pattern recognition. Over time, the AI learns what "normal" looks like for you. It sees how often you pay for design software, advertising, rides, meals, or equipment. It notices which clients pay you regularly and how much they usually send. When something changes, the system flags it. A sudden spike in income, an unusually large expense, or a missing payment does not go unnoticed. This continuous awareness creates a financial safety net that catches errors before they become expensive problems.

Income tracking is especially critical for gig workers because many platforms do not provide accurate or complete tax documents. Some only report what they process, not what you earn. Others issue 1099 forms that include refunds, fees, or even tips in ways that confuse taxpayers. AI reconciles all of this by comparing platform reports to actual deposits. If a platform claims you earned more than you received, the AI identifies the discrepancy. If income arrives without a corresponding report, the AI records it anyway so nothing is missed. This creates a complete, defensible income record that stands up to audits. Expense tracking is where AI delivers some of its biggest financial wins. Many freelancers underestimate how much they spend to make money. Small purchases feel insignificant in isolation, but they accumulate into massive deductions over a year. AI captures every one of them. Whether it is a $9.99 subscription, a $4 parking fee, or a $200 piece of equipment, the system categorizes it, stores it, and links it to your business activity. It also applies tax rules automatically, determining which expenses are fully deductible, partially deductible, or not deductible at all. This prevents both missed savings and dangerous mistakes.

One of the most powerful features of AI-driven tracking is its ability to separate personal and business finances even when they are mixed together. Many gig workers use the same credit cards and bank accounts for everything. Humans find this confusing. AI does not. It looks at transaction context, location, merchant type, and historical behavior to decide whether a purchase belongs to your business or your personal life. This makes your tax records clean even if your finances are not.

As data accumulates, AI begins to see trends that humans never notice. It identifies which platforms generate the most profit after expenses. It shows you which clients are actually worth your time. It reveals where money leaks out through inefficiency. These insights allow you to make better decisions about where to focus your energy. Tax optimization is not just about deductions; it is about structuring your entire income flow in the smartest possible way.

By the time tax season arrives, everything is already done. Income is verified. Expenses are categorized. Reports are ready. There is no scrambling, no guesswork, and no panic. The AI has been building your tax return every day, quietly and accurately. This is the future of self-employed finances: a system that never forgets, never gets tired, and never misses a dollar.

"The Digital Bookkeeper"

Ethan never thought of himself as disorganized. He knew his clients, delivered his work on time, and kept his projects in perfect order. But when it came to money, his freelance photography business was a mess. Payments came from weddings, stock photo sales, editing gigs, and social media partnerships, all landing in different accounts. He knew he was making good money, but he had no idea where it went.

Everything changed when he connected his accounts to an AI financial system. At first, it simply displayed his income in one place, and even that felt revolutionary. For the first time, he could see every dollar he earned in a single dashboard. Then it began categorizing his expenses automatically. Camera gear, software, travel, meals, and cloud storage were all labeled and sorted without him lifting a finger.

Weeks later, the AI alerted him to something strange. One of his platforms reported more income than he had actually received. He would never have noticed it on his own, but the system caught it instantly. A quick correction saved him from paying tax on money he never earned. It was the first time Ethan realized that his digital bookkeeper was not just recording his finances, it was protecting them.

As months passed, the system learned his habits. It knew which cafes he used as workspaces, which flights were business trips, and which purchases were personal. It separated everything automatically, turning chaos into order. Tax season arrived without drama. No piles of receipts. No missing statements. Just clean, organized data ready to file.

For Ethan, the biggest surprise was not how much money he saved, but how much mental space he gained. With his finances under control, he could focus on what he loved: capturing moments, telling stories, and growing his business. The AI didn't just track his money. It gave him back his peace.

Chapter 3

How AI Finds Hidden Deductions and Slashes Your Tax Bill

For gig workers and freelancers, the biggest enemy of financial success is not the IRS. It is invisibility. Most people do not lose money because they break tax rules, but because they fail to see how many rules work in their favor. The tax code is filled with deductions, credits, depreciation schedules, and business expense rules designed to support entrepreneurship. Yet these benefits are buried beneath complexity that overwhelms the average person. Artificial intelligence changes this by turning the tax code into an engine that actively searches for savings instead of one that punishes mistakes.

AI does not look at your finances the way a human does. It does not see a long list of transactions. It sees patterns, categories, and opportunities. When you buy a laptop, it recognizes not just a purchase, but a depreciable asset. When you pay for software, it recognizes an operating expense. When you travel, it breaks the cost into transportation, lodging, and meals, each with its own tax treatment. Even something as ordinary as a home internet bill becomes a potential deduction when AI recognizes that it supports your business activity. This level of detail allows the system to apply the tax code in ways that no human could sustain consistently.

One of the most powerful ways AI saves money is through classification. Every transaction is placed into the most tax-advantaged category possible based on rules, usage, and historical patterns. A meal with a client is treated differently than groceries at home. A phone purchase for business is treated differently than a personal upgrade. AI evaluates context using time, location, merchant type, and spending history. Over thousands of transactions, these small optimizations add up to thousands of dollars in legal tax savings.

Depreciation is another area where freelancers often lose money. Expensive equipment like cameras, computers, vehicles, and machinery can often be deducted over time or even expensed immediately using special tax rules. Most people either forget to apply these rules or apply them incorrectly. AI handles this automatically. It identifies assets, tracks their value, applies the correct depreciation method, and ensures that every allowed deduction is captured without risking compliance. What once required a tax professional now happens quietly in the background.

Home office deductions are one of the most misunderstood and underused tax benefits. Many gig workers believe they do not qualify because they work from a kitchen table or a spare room. AI looks at actual usage patterns, location data, and spending behavior to calculate exactly how much of your home is used for business and how much of rent, utilities, and internet can legally be deducted. This turns ordinary living expenses into powerful tax shields when applied correctly.

AI also identifies deductions that humans rarely think about. Professional education, subscriptions, web hosting, marketing tools, banking fees, and even parts of your phone bill can be deductible. Because AI monitors spending continuously, nothing slips through the cracks. It does not get tired, it does not forget, and it does not miss small purchases that add up to big money over time.

What makes this process safe is that AI applies tax rules consistently and conservatively. It does not invent deductions. It finds them within the law. It flags questionable expenses for review. It keeps documentation linked to every claim. This creates an audit-ready record that supports every dollar you deduct. You are not just saving money. You are building a fortress of compliance around your return.

The result is a tax system that works for you instead of against you. You stop guessing. You stop worrying. You stop leaving money on the table. AI transforms your finances from a source of stress into a source of strategic advantage, allowing you to grow your business while paying the lowest legal tax possible.

"The Money Maya Never Knew She Had"

When Maya looked at her tax return from last year, she felt defeated. She had worked harder than ever, but her savings barely grew. It seemed like no matter how much she earned, something always took it away. That changed the day her AI tax system showed her what had been hiding in plain sight.

It began with small things. A coffee shop she used as an office. A monthly design subscription. A portion of her rent that supported her work. One by one, the AI categorized expenses she never thought were deductible. Each time it found one, her projected tax bill dropped a little more. It felt like discovering loose change scattered throughout her life, except this time it added up to thousands.

Then it found the big ones. Her computer, her camera, her office furniture. The AI applied depreciation rules she had never heard of, spreading the cost in a way that maximized her deductions. What she once saw as expensive purchases now became strategic investments.

By midyear, Maya was no longer afraid to spend money to grow her business. The AI showed her exactly how those expenses reduced her taxes. When she invested in better equipment and advertising, her profits increased and her tax burden stayed under control. For the first time, growth did not feel dangerous.

When tax season arrived, Maya realized she was no longer just earning money. She was keeping it. The invisible drain that once haunted her was gone. Thanks to AI, she finally saw the full value of her work, and it was more than she ever imagined.

Chapter 4

Quarterly Taxes, Cash Flow, and How AI Eliminates Guesswork

For freelancers and gig workers, quarterly taxes are where financial stress quietly accumulates. Unlike employees who have taxes withheld automatically, self-employed workers must calculate, save, and submit estimated payments four times a year based on projected income. These payments are not suggestions; they are legal obligations, and getting them wrong can trigger penalties, interest, and cash-flow crises. Yet the very nature of freelance income makes accurate estimation extremely difficult. Income fluctuates, expenses change, and opportunities appear unexpectedly. Artificial intelligence exists to solve this exact problem by replacing estimation with precision.

Most freelancers either underpay or overpay their quarterly taxes. Underpayment happens when income increases unexpectedly or expenses are overestimated. Overpayment happens when freelancers play it safe and send too much money to the IRS, effectively giving the government an interest-free loan. Both outcomes hurt financial growth. AI eliminates this tradeoff by continuously recalculating tax obligations as income and expenses change. Instead of guessing what you might owe in three months, AI knows what you owe right now and projects forward with increasing accuracy.

AI forecasting works by analyzing historical income patterns, seasonal trends, platform behavior, and expense ratios. If your income spikes during certain months or drops during others, the system learns this rhythm. If a new client increases revenue, AI adjusts projections immediately. If expenses rise due to investment or expansion, tax estimates respond accordingly. This creates a living forecast rather than a static estimate, allowing freelancers to plan with confidence instead of fear.

Cash flow is inseparable from taxes in self-employment. Every dollar you earn feels available until taxes are due. Many freelancers accidentally spend money that technically belongs to the IRS, then scramble when quarterly deadlines arrive. AI prevents this by separating taxable income from usable cash in real time. It shows how much money is truly yours and how much should be reserved. This clarity transforms financial decision-making. Spending becomes intentional. Saving becomes automatic. Panic disappears.

AI also optimizes the timing of income and expenses to improve cash flow. It can recommend when to invoice clients, when to delay or accelerate expenses, and how different timing decisions affect quarterly payments. For freelancers with control over billing cycles, this insight alone can mean the difference between financial strain and financial stability. Taxes stop being a surprise and start becoming a strategic variable.

Another major advantage of AI-driven quarterly tax management is penalty prevention. The IRS penalizes taxpayers not just for underpayment, but for inconsistent payment behavior. AI tracks compliance thresholds automatically, ensuring that payments meet safe harbor rules and minimizing audit risk. Instead of relying on vague guidelines or outdated advice, freelancers operate with precise, up-to-date compliance intelligence.

AI also simplifies the act of paying quarterly taxes. It generates exact payment amounts, prepares documentation, and provides reminders before deadlines. Some systems even integrate directly with payment platforms, making submission nearly effortless. What once required calendars, spreadsheets, and anxiety now becomes a routine, low-stress process.

When quarterly taxes are handled correctly, freelancers gain something far more valuable than savings: control. They can invest confidently, expand deliberately, and plan long-term goals without fear of tax consequences. AI turns quarterly taxes from a recurring threat into a predictable, manageable system that supports growth rather than limiting it.

"The Quarter That Changed Everything"

Liam had always dreaded March, June, September, and January. Those months meant quarterly taxes, and quarterly taxes meant stress. No matter how hard he worked, those deadlines felt like ambushes. One good month would trick him into spending more, and one slow month would leave him short when payments were due. He never felt ahead, only reactive.

When Liam adopted an AI financial system, he expected organization. What he didn't expect was foresight. The system showed him not just what he earned, but what he would owe weeks and months in advance. It separated his income into usable cash and reserved tax money automatically. For the first time, he knew exactly where he stood.

As his freelance consulting business grew, the AI adapted instantly. When a new client doubled his monthly revenue, his tax reserve adjusted the same day. When he invested in software and marketing, the system recalculated his quarterly obligations automatically. There were no surprises, no last-minute scrambles, no fear.

One quarter, Liam faced a slow month and expected trouble. Instead, the AI showed him that his prior overpayment created a buffer. He paid less that quarter without penalty. Another time, the system warned him early that income growth required higher payments, giving him time to prepare. Each alert felt like a quiet rescue.

By the end of the year, Liam realized something profound. Taxes no longer dictated his behavior. He dictated his finances. Quarterly payments became routine, predictable, and manageable. What once felt like a threat now felt like a checkpoint he passed with ease.

The quarter that changed everything wasn't about earning more money. It was about finally knowing where it went—and where it needed to go.

Chapter 5

Audit Protection, Compliance, and How AI Keeps You Safe

For gig workers and freelancers, the word audit carries a weight far heavier than it should. It represents uncertainty, fear, and the possibility that years of hard work could be questioned, delayed, or undone by paperwork errors rather than wrongdoing. Most audits are not triggered by fraud. They are triggered by mismatches, inconsistencies, missing documentation, or statistical anomalies that stand out in automated IRS systems. The problem is that the modern freelancer operates in a financial environment filled with fragmentation, complexity, and human error. Artificial intelligence exists to eliminate those vulnerabilities by creating a financial record that is not only optimized, but defensible.

Compliance is not about perfection. It is about consistency. The IRS does not expect freelancers to know every rule, but it does expect numbers to align across reports, platforms, and filings. When income reported by third parties does not match what appears on a tax return, red flags appear. When deductions are claimed without documentation, risk increases. When expenses fluctuate wildly without explanation, systems notice. AI neutralizes these triggers by continuously reconciling data, applying rules consistently, and documenting every decision automatically.

One of the most powerful protections AI offers is reconciliation. Every dollar of income reported by a platform, payment processor, or client is matched against actual deposits. If a discrepancy exists, the system flags it immediately. This prevents the most common audit trigger of all: income mismatch. Instead of discovering a problem months or years later, freelancers correct issues in real time, often before returns are filed. This proactive correction alone dramatically reduces audit probability.

Documentation is the backbone of audit defense. Most freelancers do not lose audits because deductions are illegal; they lose because they cannot prove them. Receipts are missing. Logs are incomplete. Notes are vague. AI eliminates this weakness by attaching documentation to every transaction automatically. Receipts are stored, categorized, and linked. Mileage is tracked using location data. Home office calculations are supported by usage patterns. Every deduction has a digital trail that explains not just what was deducted, but why.

Consistency across time is another major compliance challenge. When deductions spike one year and disappear the next, or when expense ratios swing dramatically without explanation, it attracts attention. AI creates continuity by applying the same logic year after year. If your business grows, the system documents why. If expenses rise, it explains how. This narrative continuity is critical in audits because it shows intention rather than randomness.

AI also protects freelancers from accidental overreach. Many people unknowingly claim deductions they are not fully entitled to, not out of dishonesty, but misunderstanding. AI systems apply conservative rules by default. They flag gray areas instead of blindly deducting them. They recommend review when context is unclear. This built-in restraint is essential because the safest tax strategy is not the most aggressive one, but the most defensible one.

Another overlooked aspect of compliance is timing. Late filings, late payments, and inconsistent quarterly estimates increase scrutiny. AI manages deadlines automatically, sending alerts, preparing payment amounts, and ensuring that nothing slips through the cracks. Compliance becomes routine rather than reactive. The fewer emergencies you have, the less attention your account attracts.

Perhaps the most profound shift AI brings is psychological. Fear causes mistakes. Panic causes shortcuts. Stress causes avoidance. When freelancers know their records are clean, organized, and supported, they behave differently. They respond instead of react. They plan instead of scramble. This calm consistency is reflected in filings, behavior, and outcomes.

AI does not make you invisible to the IRS, nor should it. Instead, it makes you uninteresting. Clean numbers, aligned reports, documented deductions, and predictable behavior are the hallmarks of low-risk taxpayers. This is not about hiding. It is about clarity. And clarity is the strongest form of protection.

"The Letter That Never Came"

Noah had been self-employed for eight years, and for eight years he lived with a quiet, constant fear. It never screamed, never interrupted his work, but it followed him everywhere. Every email from the government made his stomach tighten. Every tax season brought sleepless nights. He had never done anything wrong, but he had also never felt safe.

His income came from everywhere. Consulting clients wired payments. Platforms deposited weekly. Royalties arrived quarterly. Expenses were scattered across cards, apps, and accounts. He did his best to track everything, but deep down he knew it wasn't perfect. Something was always missing.

Something was always guessed. He told himself it was normal. Everyone did it this way.

Then one afternoon, a fellow freelancer mentioned an AI system that handled tax compliance automatically. Noah was skeptical. He didn't want aggressive deductions or risky tricks. He wanted peace. He wanted to know that if someone ever asked questions, he would have answers.

The first thing the AI did was unsettling. It showed him inconsistencies he didn't know existed. Platform income that didn't perfectly match deposits. Expenses that were duplicated. Deductions that lacked receipts. It wasn't accusatory. It was calm. Clinical. Honest. And for the first time, Noah saw his finances the way an auditor might.

Week by week, the system cleaned everything. Receipts were attached. Categories were clarified. Income sources were reconciled. When something didn't align, it flagged it early. When a deduction was questionable, it asked for confirmation instead of assuming. Slowly, the fear began to loosen its grip.

Months later, something unexpected happened. Noah received a notice from one of the platforms correcting a prior income report. In the past, this would have sent him into panic. This time, the AI had already flagged the issue, adjusted the records, and documented the explanation. There was nothing to do. Nothing to fix. Nothing to fear. As years passed, Noah noticed something else. He stopped thinking about audits entirely. His filings were consistent. His payments were timely. His records were complete. He wasn't hiding. He wasn't overreaching. He was simply operating with clarity.

One tax season, friends began receiving audit letters. Group chats filled with panic. Noah waited for his. Days passed. Weeks passed. Months passed. It never came.

The absence of that letter became the loudest confirmation he had ever received.

Noah realized then that freedom wasn't just earning money on your own terms. It was knowing that your past was as clean as your present. The AI hadn't just protected his taxes. It had given him back something he didn't realize he had lost.

Silence.

And in that silence, Noah finally felt safe.

Chapter 6

Scaling Income Without Scaling Taxes: How AI Turns Growth Into an Advantage

For gig workers and freelancers, growth is often treated as a double-edged sword. Earning more money sounds like success, but higher income frequently brings higher taxes, larger quarterly payments, and increased financial pressure. Many self-employed individuals unconsciously limit their growth because they fear the tax consequences of success. This fear is not irrational. Without intelligent systems in place, scaling income can indeed feel punishing. Artificial intelligence exists to reverse this dynamic by ensuring that growth increases efficiency, not stress.

The core problem is that most freelancers scale revenue before they scale systems. Income rises quickly, but tracking, planning, and compliance lag behind. Expenses increase, deductions are missed, and quarterly payments are miscalculated. The result is a larger tax bill without a proportional increase in retained income. AI changes this by scaling alongside income automatically. As revenue grows, AI adjusts categorization, forecasting, deduction strategies, and compliance thresholds in real time. Growth becomes structured rather than chaotic.

One of the most powerful ways AI supports scalable tax efficiency is by revealing the true cost of growth. Not all income is equal. Some clients are highly profitable, while others generate revenue that disappears into expenses and taxes. AI analyzes profit margins by client, platform, and service type, allowing freelancers to focus on income that produces the highest after-tax returns. This insight shifts decision-making from "How do I earn more?" to "How do I keep more?"

As income grows, entity structure becomes increasingly important. Many freelancers remain sole proprietors long after it stops being tax-efficient. AI models income thresholds, expense ratios, and tax outcomes to determine when forming an LLC, electing S-corporation status, or restructuring compensation becomes beneficial. Instead of guessing or relying on generic advice, freelancers receive personalized guidance based on their actual financial data. This ensures that structural changes happen at the right time, not too early and not too late.

AI also optimizes reinvestment. Growth often requires spending money on tools, marketing, education, contractors, and infrastructure. These investments reduce taxable income when timed and categorized correctly. AI simulates reinvestment scenarios, showing how spending decisions affect taxes, cash flow, and long-term profitability. This transforms reinvestment from a leap of faith into a calculated strategy. Freelancers gain the confidence to grow because they understand the tax impact before money is spent.

Another critical advantage of AI-driven scaling is cash-flow protection. Rapid growth can paradoxically create liquidity problems if tax reserves are not adjusted properly. AI continuously separates usable cash from tax obligations as income rises. This prevents the common mistake of reinvesting money that should be reserved for taxes. Growth remains sustainable because obligations are always visible.

AI also helps freelancers avoid lifestyle inflation traps. As income increases, spending often increases just as quickly. AI highlights how personal spending affects business cash flow and tax efficiency. It creates awareness without judgment, allowing freelancers to make intentional choices instead of reactive ones. This awareness is essential for turning higher income into lasting wealth rather than temporary comfort.

The ultimate goal of scaling is not just earning more, but building resilience. AI enables freelancers to grow without fear because it provides visibility, foresight, and structure at every stage. Growth stops feeling dangerous and starts feeling rewarding. Taxes become a managed variable, not an unpredictable threat. With AI, scaling income is no longer about working harder. It is about working smarter and keeping control as success expands.

"The Year Everything Accelerated"

The year Elena's income doubled was the year she almost quit freelancing.

At least, that was how it felt halfway through. On paper, she was more successful than she had ever been. Her consulting calendar was full. Clients recommended her constantly. Deposits arrived daily. Yet somehow, she felt poorer, more anxious, and more exhausted than before. Every new client came with excitement followed by dread. More income meant more taxes, more uncertainty, and more pressure she couldn't quite explain.

At night, Elena lay awake doing mental math. She tried to guess how much she owed. She tried to estimate how much she could safely spend. She tried to remember whether she had saved enough for quarterly payments. The numbers never felt solid. They floated, shifting with every new invoice and every new expense. Growth felt like running faster on unstable ground. It was during one of those sleepless nights that she connected her finances to an AI tax system recommended by a colleague. She expected organization. What she didn't expect was clarity. The dashboard didn't just show income. It showed retained income. It separated what belonged to her from what belonged to future obligations. For the first time, Elena saw growth broken down into truth instead of illusion.

As weeks passed, the system began revealing patterns she had never noticed. Some clients looked lucrative but drained her time and expenses. Others produced fewer invoices but far higher margins. The AI quietly ranked them, not by revenue, but by after-tax profit. Elena realized she had been chasing volume instead of value.

Then came the turning point. The AI flagged that her income had crossed a threshold where her current structure was no longer efficient. It simulated alternatives. The numbers were unmistakable. With a simple structural change and adjusted compensation strategy, her tax burden dropped dramatically. The same income. Less stress. More retained cash.

Elena hesitated at first. Change felt risky. But the system showed her the path step by step. Nothing aggressive. Nothing rushed. Just precision. When she made the shift, the effect was immediate. Quarterly payments stabilized. Cash reserves grew. Growth stopped feeling like a threat.

Midyear, Elena reinvested. Better software. Strategic advertising. A virtual assistant. Each decision felt intentional because she saw the tax impact before spending. The AI showed her how reinvestment reduced taxable income while expanding capacity. Growth became strategic instead of reactive.

As the year accelerated, something subtle changed inside her. She stopped fearing success. She stopped bracing for impact every time income increased. She trusted the numbers because they were no longer guesses. They were living data, adjusting in real time.

By year's end, Elena looked back at the version of herself who almost quit and barely recognized her. Not because she worked harder, but because she finally understood her growth. The AI hadn't created her success. It had made her success sustainable.

And for the first time, Elena welcomed acceleration instead of fearing it — because she knew exactly where she was going, and exactly how much she would keep when she arrived.

Chapter 7

From Survival to Strategy: How AI Transforms Freelancers Into Long-Term Wealth Builders

Most gig workers and freelancers begin their journey focused on survival. The initial goal is simple: replace income, pay bills, stay afloat. Taxes are treated as an unavoidable nuisance rather than a strategic component of financial life. This mindset is not a flaw; it is a natural response to uncertainty. However, remaining in survival mode for too long becomes costly. Without a long-term strategy, income fluctuates wildly, taxes feel punitive, and wealth never fully accumulates. Artificial intelligence marks the transition point between survival and strategy by turning daily financial activity into a cohesive long-term plan.

The difference between surviving and thriving lies in intention. Surviving freelancers react to money as it comes and goes. Strategic freelancers shape how money moves through their lives. AI enables this shift by connecting short-term actions to long-term outcomes. Every invoice, expense, investment, and tax payment becomes part of a larger financial narrative rather than an isolated event. This narrative view is essential for wealth building because it reveals patterns that only emerge over time.

One of the most powerful strategic advantages AI provides is future modeling. Instead of asking, "How much will I owe this year?" freelancers begin asking, "What happens if I earn this much for the next five years?" AI simulates multiple futures based on income growth, reinvestment choices, tax strategies, and lifestyle decisions. This allows freelancers to choose paths deliberately rather than stumbling into outcomes by accident. Wealth becomes a destination, not a coincidence.

Taxes play a central role in this transformation. For strategic freelancers, taxes are no longer just obligations; they are planning tools. AI shows how retirement contributions, reinvestment timing, entity structures, and income smoothing affect long-term outcomes. Instead of minimizing taxes in isolation, freelancers optimize taxes in harmony with cash flow, growth, and personal goals. This integrated approach is what turns high income into lasting wealth.

AI also helps freelancers escape the "feast or famine" cycle that traps many self-employed workers. By analyzing income volatility and expense behavior, it recommends buffers, reserves, and pacing strategies that stabilize finances across years, not just months. Stability is a prerequisite for wealth because it allows consistent investing, long-term planning, and emotional clarity. Without stability, even high earners struggle to build anything lasting.

Another strategic shift enabled by AI is the separation of identity from income. Many freelancers tie their sense of security directly to monthly earnings. AI introduces a broader perspective by tracking net worth, retained earnings, and long-term progress. This reduces emotional dependence on short-term fluctuations and encourages decisions that favor sustainability over immediate gratification.

As freelancers mature financially, AI evolves with them. It begins coordinating tax strategy with retirement planning, asset acquisition, and wealth protection. It highlights opportunities to diversify income, reduce risk, and preserve gains. At this stage, taxes are no longer feared or avoided. They are understood, anticipated, and optimized as part of a larger system.

Ultimately, AI transforms freelancing from a hustle into an enterprise. It replaces anxiety with clarity, reaction with intention, and effort with leverage. Survival becomes strategy. Income becomes wealth. And taxes, once a source of fear, become one of the most powerful tools in the freelancer's financial arsenal.

"The Long View"

For most of his freelance career, Daniel lived one month at a time. He didn't plan that way intentionally; it simply felt necessary. Some months were good, others were lean, and every decision revolved around the next invoice. Taxes existed in the background like a storm cloud he preferred not to look at directly. He paid what he owed when deadlines arrived and tried not to think beyond that.

Daniel told himself this was normal. Freelancing was unpredictable by nature, he reasoned. Stability was for people with salaries, not for someone who built income from projects, clients, and creativity. Yet year after year, something bothered him. Despite earning more than he ever had before, his financial position barely changed. Money moved through his hands, but it didn't seem to stay.

The realization came quietly, not during a crisis, but during a calm moment. Daniel reviewed his finances one evening and saw that five years of work had left him almost exactly where he started. More experienced. More tired. Not much wealthier. It wasn't failure, but it wasn't success either. It was motion without progress.

That was when he decided to try an AI financial system designed for freelancers. He didn't expect miracles. He wanted insight. The first thing the system showed him wasn't comforting, but it was honest. It displayed his financial life as a timeline, not a balance. Patterns appeared instantly. Income spikes followed by spending spikes. Tax payments that disrupted momentum. Years where growth occurred but retention didn't.

Instead of overwhelming him, the AI slowed everything down. It asked better questions than Daniel had ever asked himself. What did he want his income to support long term? How much stability did he actually need? What would happen if he made slightly different decisions consistently over several years instead of chasing short-term comfort?

For the first time, Daniel saw projections that extended beyond the current year. Five years. Ten years. Different versions of his future unfolded on the screen. One path led to continued volatility and stress. Another led to steady growth, stronger reserves, and meaningful investments. The difference wasn't dramatic changes. It was small, repeatable adjustments guided by awareness.

Taxes became part of the story rather than interruptions. The AI showed how strategic reinvestment lowered tax burden while increasing capacity. How retirement contributions compounded quietly. How pacing income prevented burnout and stabilized cash flow. Each decision made sense because it connected to something larger.

Months passed, then years. Daniel didn't suddenly feel rich. What he felt was grounded. Calm. Confident. When income dipped, he didn't panic. When income surged, he didn't rush to spend. He understood where he was, where he was going, and why.

One evening, Daniel looked at his financial dashboard and noticed something subtle but powerful. His net worth had grown steadily, quietly, without drama. Not because he worked harder, but because he finally worked with intention. Survival had given way to strategy.

He realized then that freelancing hadn't failed him. He had simply never taken the long view. And once he did, everything changed.

Chapter 8

Automation, Peace of Mind, and the End of Tax Anxiety

Tax anxiety is one of the most underestimated burdens carried by freelancers and gig workers. It does not always announce itself as panic or fear. Often, it lives quietly in the background as avoidance, procrastination, vague unease, or constant second-guessing. It shows up when income increases but confidence does not. It appears when spending money feels risky even when business is thriving. This anxiety is not caused by taxes themselves, but by uncertainty. Artificial intelligence exists to remove that uncertainty by transforming taxes from an unpredictable threat into an automated, predictable system.

Most freelancers do not fear paying taxes. They fear not knowing whether they are doing it correctly. They fear mistakes they cannot see, deadlines they might forget, and consequences they do not fully understand. Traditional tax tools address filing, but they do not address this emotional burden. AI changes the relationship entirely by providing continuous awareness. Instead of taxes being something that happens to you once a year, they become something you understand every day. Automation is the foundation of this transformation. AI removes the need for constant decision-making by handling repetitive, rules-based tasks automatically. Income is tracked without manual entry. Expenses are categorized without guesswork. Deductions are applied consistently. Deadlines are monitored continuously. When systems run quietly in the background, mental energy is freed. The mind no longer needs to carry unfinished financial tasks. This is where peace of mind begins.

AI also replaces fear with feedback. Instead of wondering whether you are on track, you can see it. Instead of hoping you saved enough, you know. Instead of reacting to surprises, you receive early warnings. This feedback loop creates trust, not just in the system, but in yourself. Confidence grows because decisions are supported by data rather than intuition alone.

Another critical aspect of peace of mind is simplicity. Freelancers often juggle multiple tools, spreadsheets, apps, and reminders. This fragmentation creates stress even when things are technically under control. AI consolidates everything into a single, coherent system. One source of truth replaces many partial ones. This clarity reduces cognitive overload and restores focus.

Automation also reduces emotional volatility. When taxes are managed manually, every income spike can trigger anxiety and every expense can feel like a gamble. AI smooths these emotional swings by contextualizing every transaction within a larger plan. Money stops feeling fragile and starts feeling structured. This emotional stability is essential for long-term success because it prevents burnout and impulsive decisions.

Over time, automated tax systems reshape identity. Freelancers stop seeing themselves as people who "deal with taxes" and start seeing themselves as operators of intelligent financial systems. This shift is subtle but powerful. Responsibility does not disappear; it becomes lighter because it is shared with technology designed to carry it consistently.

Ultimately, AI does not remove taxes from your life. It removes fear from your relationship with them. When systems are reliable, visible, and automated, anxiety fades naturally. What remains is clarity, calm, and the ability to focus on work, creativity, and growth. This is the true promise of automation: not convenience, but peace.

"When Silence Replaced the Noise"

For years, Sofia lived with a low hum of anxiety that never quite went away. It wasn't loud enough to stop her from working, but it was constant enough to shape every decision she made. Every payment that landed in her account came with a question she couldn't answer confidently. How much of this is really mine? How much should I save? What am I forgetting?

She told herself it was part of freelancing. Everyone felt this way, she assumed. Uncertainty was the price of independence. But the truth was that the uncertainty followed her everywhere. It crept into vacations, into weekends, into moments that should have felt restful. Even when she wasn't working, her mind replayed financial "what ifs" she couldn't resolve.

Tax season was the loudest moment of the year. Papers scattered across her desk. Accounts half-remembered. Receipts she hoped she hadn't lost. She filed on time, paid what was calculated, and then waited. Waited for confirmation. Waited for relief. Waited for the next cycle to begin. The silence afterward never lasted.

Everything began to change the day Sofia connected her finances to an AI system designed for freelancers. At first, it felt intrusive. Seeing everything laid out so clearly was uncomfortable. Patterns she hadn't noticed before appeared instantly. Income volatility. Spending habits. Months where she earned more but saved less. It wasn't judgmental. It was simply accurate.

The first few weeks were noisy. Notifications. Alerts. Suggestions. Sofia worried that adding another system would increase her stress. But then something unexpected happened. The noise began to fade. Not because the system stopped working, but because it stopped surprising her. Every question she used to carry was answered before it formed fully in her mind.

She no longer wondered how much she owed. The number was there. She no longer feared missing deadlines. They were tracked automatically. She no longer guessed whether an expense was deductible. It was already categorized and documented. Slowly, the background hum quieted.

Months passed. Sofia noticed changes she hadn't anticipated. She slept better. She took days off without checking her accounts. She invested in her business without fear because she understood the impact immediately. Money stopped feeling like something that could betray her at any moment.

One evening, she realized she hadn't thought about taxes in weeks. Not avoided them. Not suppressed worry. Simply hadn't needed to think about them. The system handled what once consumed her attention. Silence had replaced noise.

A year later, Sofia looked back at the version of herself who lived in constant low-grade anxiety and felt compassion rather than frustration. She hadn't been irresponsible. She had simply lacked visibility. Automation hadn't made her careless. It had made her calm. The greatest gift AI gave her wasn't savings, efficiency, or compliance. It was mental space. And in that space, Sofia finally felt free — not just to work, but to live.

Chapter 9

Wealth Protection, Legacy Thinking, and How AI Preserves What You Build

For most freelancers and gig workers, the idea of wealth feels abstract for far too long. Income arrives, expenses leave, taxes intervene, and whatever remains is treated as temporary. The focus stays on earning rather than preserving, on movement rather than accumulation. Yet true financial success is not defined by how much money passes through your hands, but by how much stays, grows, and survives over time. Artificial intelligence enables this shift by extending financial thinking beyond income and taxes into protection, longevity, and legacy.

Wealth protection begins with visibility. You cannot protect what you cannot see clearly. AI consolidates income, expenses, taxes, savings, investments, and liabilities into a unified view that reveals net worth rather than just cash flow. This is a critical transition. Cash flow sustains life; net worth sustains freedom. Freelancers often earn well but fail to build durable assets because they lack systems that translate income into retained value. AI bridges this gap by continuously tracking what you keep, not just what you earn. One of the most powerful ways AI protects wealth is through risk identification.

Freelancers face unique vulnerabilities: income volatility, lack of employer benefits, inconsistent insurance coverage, and exposure to legal or tax-related disruptions. AI analyzes patterns and flags concentration risks, such as dependence on a single client or platform. It highlights weak points in cash reserves, identifies exposure to unexpected tax obligations, and surfaces gaps in financial protection before they become crises.

Tax strategy plays a foundational role in wealth preservation. Paying taxes correctly is not enough; paying them strategically is essential. AI coordinates tax planning with long-term goals, showing how decisions today affect future wealth. It models the impact of retirement contributions, reinvestment strategies, and timing decisions on lifetime tax burden. This transforms taxes from an annual obligation into a lifelong planning variable that can be optimized over decades.

AI also supports asset diversification, a cornerstone of wealth protection. Freelancers often reinvest solely into their own labor, upgrading tools, skills, and marketing while neglecting broader asset accumulation. AI highlights opportunities to redirect surplus income into diversified vehicles such as retirement accounts, investment portfolios, or income-producing assets. By showing projected outcomes across multiple paths, it encourages balanced growth rather than overreliance on active income. Another critical dimension of wealth protection is durability. Freelancers are especially vulnerable to burnout, health issues, or market shifts that can interrupt income. AI helps build durability by encouraging reserves, smoothing income cycles, and pacing growth sustainably. Wealth that depends on constant output is fragile. Wealth supported by systems, buffers, and automation is resilient.

Legacy thinking is the final evolution of financial maturity. It moves beyond personal comfort toward continuity, impact, and transferability. AI introduces this perspective naturally by tracking long-term trends and projecting outcomes beyond the present moment. Freelancers begin asking not just how to earn and save, but how to preserve and pass on what they build. Estate considerations, business continuity, and long-term asset protection become part of the conversation, not afterthoughts.

Ultimately, AI transforms freelancing from a temporary income strategy into a lifelong wealth-building framework. It protects against loss, inefficiency, and short-term thinking. It aligns daily decisions with long-term preservation. And it ensures that what you build does not disappear quietly, but endures with intention.

"The Things That Stayed"

For most of her career, Rachel believed that stability was something freelancers simply didn't have. She accepted volatility as the price of independence and learned to live with constant motion. Projects came and went. Income rose and fell. Money passed through her hands quickly, never staying long enough to feel permanent. She told herself that movement meant progress.

Years passed, and Rachel became highly successful by most external measures. Her calendar was full. Her reputation was strong. Her income was impressive. Yet one evening, while reviewing her finances, she noticed something unsettling. Despite all the work, all the years, and all the effort, very little had accumulated. There were no meaningful reserves. No long-term structure. Just momentum.

The realization wasn't dramatic. It was quiet, almost gentle. Rachel wasn't failing. She was simply building something that evaporated as quickly as it formed. She began to wonder what would remain if she slowed down, stepped away, or faced an unexpected interruption. The answer unsettled her.

When Rachel adopted an AI-driven financial system, she expected organization. What she received instead was perspective. The system didn't just show her balances. It showed her trajectory. It mapped her financial life across years, revealing patterns she had never noticed. High income followed by high outflow. Periods of growth without retention. Motion without permanence.

At first, the clarity was uncomfortable. Rachel felt exposed, not judged, but seen. The AI highlighted vulnerabilities she had ignored. Dependence on a small number of clients. Minimal reserves. A tax strategy that focused on compliance but not preservation. It didn't alarm her. It simply waited, offering insight when she was ready to listen.

Slowly, Rachel began making small changes. She redirected a portion of income into long-term accounts. She built reserves intentionally instead of reactively. She adjusted her tax strategy to support retention rather than just filing accuracy. None of the changes felt dramatic. They felt quiet, almost boring. But they felt right.

Over time, something remarkable happened. Rachel's financial life slowed down. Not in activity, but in urgency. She no longer felt chased by income. She wasn't afraid of slow months. She stopped measuring success solely by what arrived and started measuring it by what stayed.

One year, she took extended time off without panic. Another year, she turned down projects that paid well but drained her energy. Each decision was supported by the knowledge that she was no longer building something fragile. She was building something durable.

As the years passed, Rachel began thinking beyond herself. She thought about continuity. About what she wanted her work to support long after she stepped back. The AI reflected this shift, showing her not just projections for income, but projections for impact. For sustainability. For transferability.

One evening, Rachel reviewed her financial dashboard and smiled softly. It wasn't flashy. It wasn't dramatic. But it was solid. What she had built was no longer fleeting. It endured.

For the first time in her freelance life, Rachel understood that wealth wasn't about how fast money moved.

It was about the things that stayed.

Final Thoughts

The End of Tax Fear and the Beginning of Financial Control

The journey through this book has not been about learning tax rules, memorizing deductions, or becoming a financial expert. It has been about transformation. Specifically, the transformation from uncertainty to clarity, from reaction to intention, and from short-term survival to long-term control. For gig workers and freelancers, taxes have historically represented confusion and vulnerability. Artificial intelligence changes that relationship permanently.

When taxes are handled manually, they dominate mental space. They interrupt creativity, distort decision-making, and create unnecessary fear around growth. Many freelancers do not realize how much of their energy is consumed by what they *don't* know about their finances. AI removes that burden by making the invisible visible. It replaces guessing with knowing. It replaces fear with foresight.

Throughout this book, you have seen how AI tracks income across fragmented platforms, captures deductions that would otherwise be lost, manages quarterly payments with precision, protects against audits through consistency, scales intelligently alongside growth, and ultimately preserves wealth for the long term. These are not isolated benefits. They compound. Each system reinforces the others, creating a financial environment where stability emerges naturally.

One of the most powerful realizations for freelancers is that financial stress is not a requirement of independence. It is a symptom of missing systems. Once systems exist, stress dissolves. Confidence takes its place. Decisions become calmer, more rational, and more aligned with long-term goals. This shift is subtle, but it changes everything.

Artificial intelligence does not remove responsibility from your financial life. It strengthens it. By handling complexity reliably, AI allows you to focus on judgment, creativity, and vision rather than paperwork and worry. You remain in control, but you are no longer carrying the weight alone. This partnership between human intention and machine precision is the future of personal finance.

The true power of AI is not in automation alone, but in continuity. It does not forget what happened last month, last year, or five years ago. It builds memory into your financial life. That memory creates context, and context creates wisdom. Over time, your financial decisions become less reactive and more strategic because they are informed by patterns rather than impulses.

As a freelancer or gig worker, you are already operating in the future of work. It only makes sense to operate in the future of finance as well. The systems described in this book are not luxuries reserved for large corporations. They are tools that finally level the playing field, giving individuals access to intelligence that was once out of reach.

The end of this book is not an ending at all. It is a transition point. A moment where taxes stop being something you endure and start being something you understand. Where income stops feeling fragile and starts feeling structured. Where growth stops feeling dangerous and starts feeling intentional.

When fear is removed, possibility expands. When clarity replaces confusion, confidence follows. And when systems support your work, freedom becomes sustainable.

That is the promise of AI-powered personal tax optimization.

www.ingramcontent.com/pod-product-compliance
Lightning Source LLC
LaVergne TN
LVHW022028200926
848481LV00007B/2586
9798295586040